EVANGELICALS AND

When Baptists Disagree

edited by

MICHAEL I. BOCHENSKI

BAPTIST UNION OF GREAT BRITAIN
1993

ISBN 1 898077 50 9

British Library Cataloguing-in-publication data: catalogue record for this book is available from the British Library.

Registered address: Baptist Union of Great Britain,
Baptist House, PO Box 44, 129 Broadway, Didcot, OX11 8RT

EVANGELICALS AND ECUMENISM

When Baptists Disagree

CONTENTS

CONTRIBUTORS

The Revd Robert J. M. Amess BA
Senior Minister, Duke Street Baptist Church, Richmond, Surrey
and author of *Evangelicals and Unity*, (Kingsway 1988)

The Revd John F. Balchin BD MTh PhD
Senior Minister, Purley Baptist Church, Surrey

The Revd Michael I. Bochenski MA
Senior Minister, Dagnall Street Baptist Church, St Albans, Herts.

Mrs Faith W. Bowers BA MPhil
Member, Bloomsbury Central Baptist Church, London
and Sub-Editor, Baptist Historical Society

The Revd David R. Coffey BA
General Secretary, Baptist Union of Great Britain

The Revd Andrew Rigden-Green BA
Senior Minister, Upton Vale Baptist Church, Torquay, Devon

The Revd Douglas G. T. McBain BD
General Superintendent, Metropolitan Area, Baptist Union

TOWARDS AN EVANGELICAL
THEOLOGY OF ECUMENISM (1)

INTRODUCTION

'We have seen his star in the east and have come to worship him'. So said the most famous of Biblical pilgrims - clearly kept united by their objective reference point in the sky. Unfortunately such clear guidance eludes many travellers on the ecumenical path. Coming from many Christian traditions, that unifying star seems to be missing. Evangelical Christians, on the other hand, span many denominations and yet claim a common reference point. Their perspective on the ecumenical debate, therefore, needs to be heard because it could bring a healthy realism into the whole debate.

The fundamental thesis of this paper is that talk of the church (ecclesiology) is not divorced from a fundamental knowledge of God (theology). Indeed, key theological truths about revelation, Christ, salvation and the church form a chain of ideas with several links. Each truth is dependent on the other and forms a whole. For this reason questions of church unity cannot be cut out as though they were just a matter of structures and organisation. Rather, issues that concern the church concern God and the way we understand him. The issues raised by the ecumenical movement go to the heart of Christian truth.

DEFINING AN EVANGELICAL THEOLOGY

Evangelicals claim to be merely orthodox Christians who stand in the mainstream of the historic witness to Christ. There is, therefore, no party creed - but the historic creeds of Athanasius and Nicaea; there is no party line but what is evident in Scripture. Nevertheless, there have been many attempts at defining evangelicalism. David Bebbington's definition is deduced from history. He sees it as 'conversionism, activism, biblicism, crucicentrism'. John Stott, one of the greatest evangelical leaders this century, says 'the hallmark of authentic evangelicalism has always been a zeal for the honour and glory of Jesus Christ'. In other words, there are key emphases within the overall Biblical witness which evangelicals have picked up and which can be seen today.

The definitions above give four theological themes:

1. **Epistemology** (theories of knowledge and authority)

Evangelicals believe that we know God only because he has chosen to reveal himself. There is a general revelation in creation and in the conscience of humankind. However, God's special revelation is in Christ (the Word made flesh) and we encounter him uniquely through the written word (the Bible). For Evangelicals, Scripture has a special place since it leads to a knowledge of God. Whereas other traditions may see the source of authority in tradition (the Catholic view) or reason (the liberal view), Evangelicals claim supreme authority to be in the Scriptures which reveal Christ.

2. **Christology** (a doctrine of Christ)

Evangelical Christology is thoroughly orthodox. In this sense it would be difficult to claim that our treatment of Christ is distinctly different from that of other traditions. Every Christian tradition would claim to put Christ at the centre of their worship and their credal statements. However, there is an evangelical distinctiveness in the way the uniqueness of Christ is upheld. He is not just *one* way of salvation, but the *only way* of salvation. He is not just a revelation of God, but *the revelation* of God. Christ is therefore the focus of doctrines of Revelation and Salvation.

3. **Soteriology** (a doctrine of salvation)

The Reformers spoke of salvation by grace through faith in Christ. These tenets of the Reformation have become watchwords for Evangelicals. They have both a negative and positive impact. Negatively they declare that salvation is not a matter of good works, or of birth to the right family, or of some religious and sacramental rite. Positively, salvation is understood as entirely God's gracious work appropriated by an individual's faith in the completed work of Christ.

4. **Ecclesiology** (a doctrine of the church)

If an Evangelical were asked who were members of the true church of Christ, he/she would reply 'Those people past, present and future who have received salvation through faith in Christ are members of the holy catholic church'. Christians in other traditions may define the church in other ways. For example, they may point to the structure of authority through the succession of bishops. Others may look to specific 'marks of the church', such as the presence of the sacraments, the Scriptures, authority and discipline. These other views of the nature of the church are important; nevertheless it is still possible to have both these 'true marks' of the church and proper structures of authority - but still have no people with saving faith. The Evangelical stresses that saving faith in the hearts of the believers is the basis for the existence of the church. For Baptists, the church is defined as the 'gathered community' of those with saving faith. Such an 'assembly' (a better translation of the word *ekklesia*) does not need the authority of any person or body outside itself. Each local gathering of believers is that visible expression of the Body of Christ.

ECCLESIOLOGY AND A THEOLOGY OF ECUMENISM

It should be evident from the above view of evangelical theology that ecclesiology is inextricably linked with soteriology, Christology and epistemology. These are all links in a chain which cannot be broken. Thus when we speak of the church we are also making assumptions about other truths. We must be assuming that the church is . . .

1. The 'believing' church

This is the most obvious corollary of an evangelical (and especially Baptist) view of the church. The church can only be made up of believers. Baptism is therefore that sign of personal faith in Christ. We speak of 'believer's baptism' for that same reason. It is not adult baptism - because an adult may not be a believer. Nor is it infant baptism - because a baby is incapable of personal faith. Ecumenical debate therefore cannot side-step this essential issue of personal faith in Christ. We are not primarily interested in the credentials of bishops, or the way the sacraments are administered. What we want to know is: do other 'assemblies' put personal faith in Christ as *the* most significant factor in the being of the church?

2. The church that believes

Since we define the very existence of a church by the members' personal faith in Christ, it is obvious that the church has to believe in a certain body of truth. It is a commitment to and trust in truth that brings life to an individual and brings birth to a church. Put quite simply, truth matters to the church. If some regard Christ, therefore, as one among several saviours, or if it is thought that there are other ways to God, then we are talking about a sort of Christianity with which no Evangelical can be happy. Evangelical theology demands that Truth be taken very seriously. Ecumenical dialogue cannot talk about the church as though the issue were divorced from questions of doctrinal truth. The church only exists because of Christian truth, so the two must be discussed together.

3. The church that is essentially local

If the church is regarded as a 'gathering of believers' in a specific locality, then supra-local structures have to be viewed with caution. The Baptist Union is merely the confederation of many local churches; the Union is not The Church. Thus conversations between denominational officers cannot be said to be 'dialogue between the churches', but merely conversations between representatives from the churches. Again, the present ecumenical movement has confused some Evangelicals and they need to take stock. The autonomy of the local church should be respected by those who represent our churches. Such representatives must recognise that they cannot make a decision for The Church.

EVANGELICAL THEOLOGY AND A SPIRIT OF OPEN-NESS

So far we have shown that an evangelical theology will necessarily have important implications for a theology of ecumenism. Our central thesis is that questions of basic Christian truth are crucial to any understanding of the church. Any scheme for church unity cannot side-step questions of fundamental doctrine. The problem with this stance is that it may look belligerent and unyielding, as though there is nothing Evangelicals can learn from other traditions. There are, however, at least three theological truths that should help to guard us against such arrogance.

1. A doctrine of a dynamic Holy Spirit

The Book of Acts is full of instances when the Holy Spirit does the unexpected. For example, Cornelius, the outsider, is told by the Spirit to come to Peter (Acts 10). Again, it is the Holy Spirit who sends out Paul and Barnabas in missionary service (Acts 13). No group of Christians can say they have captured the Holy Spirit in such a way that he cannot surprise them with and by new things. Evangelicals holding a high view of Scripture should be particularly aware of the dynamic work of the Spirit in the interpretation of the Word. The writer to the Hebrews says that Scripture is like a two-edged sword which cuts into us. The Holy Spirit causes us to see ourselves as God sees us, not as we see ourselves through our cultural spectacles. Every Christian has got to fight the desire to master Scripture and, rather, allow Scripture to master us. This means that there will always be new things unfolding from God's word - particularly as it relates to our changing culture. Partnership with other traditions may supply those helpful insights and we must be open to them.

2. A doctrine of a diverse Body of Christ

When Paul used the body metaphor in 1 Corinthians 12, he intended to convey the sense of legitimate diversity. The foot is clearly different from the hand, says Paul, and although he applies this particularly to diversities of ministry, there are surely wider applications. For example: a variety of forms of worship (1 Cor 14) and of types of leadership (Eph 4). Paul also accepted that there were some issues (e.g., what could legitimately be eaten, as in Romans 14) upon which there could be a legitimate diversity of opinion. It is also clear that he practised different methods of evangelism depending on the culture and people (compare Acts 17 with Acts 14). Moreover, it is clear that Paul recognised that different situations brought about churches with different characters. Thus, on the question of freedom from the law, Paul deals with the Galatians in a way different from his dealings with the Corinthians. We must go still further and say that the whole witness of Scripture itself is a testimony to legitimate diversity. The character and background of every Biblical author gives each letter or book its own distinctiveness. Thus, there is a discernible difference between the theological expression of Paul and the theological expression of John and of the writer to the Hebrews.

3. A doctrine of a fallen humanity

Paul tells us to 'make every effort to keep the unity of the Spirit in the bond of peace' (Eph 4:3). This appeal reveals the reality of church life. Although we already have a one-ness in truth, our fallen human nature is such that we will always be falling short of God's standard. Pride and selfishness will always be causing problems within and between churches.

In particular Jesus again and again draws our attention to the particular perversity of religious sin/s which makes people so pompous and so blind (e.g., Matt 23:24). A proper understanding of the fallenness of humanity will always make the Christian humble in his/her personal assessment, and respectful of and open to the guidance of others.

EVANGELICAL THEOLOGY AND THE BOUNDS OF LEGITIMATE DIVERSITY

There is no doubt that the New Testament speaks of some legitimate diversity in the expression of the truths of God. Today we know that forms of worship, church government and Christian life-style vary enormously according to age and culture. Many of these differences are seen in New Testament times and are regarded as legitimate expressions of fundamental truths. No such sense of legitimacy, however, is given to those who deviate from central truths of the Gospel. Jude sees that 'the faith that was once for all entrusted to the saints' does not change and cannot be adapted. Paul says that any other 'gospel' which differs from the apostolic gospel is no gospel at all (Gal 1:7)! For this reason Paul is prepared to jeopardise even the unity of the church - for the sake of Gospel truth. No careful reader of Paul's epistles can fail to realise that ultimately the truth of the Gospel was more important than a unity that seemed good only on the surface. For Paul realised that true unity within the church had to be based on firmer foundations than warm feelings and goodwill. Only a unity in truth would count. So when Jesus prays for the disciples (John 17), he prays specifically that the Father might 'sanctify them in the truth'. In any ecumenical endeavour, there can be no more basic prayer.

EVANGELICAL THEOLOGY AND THE PRESENT ECUMENICAL DEBATE

The inter-connection between ecclesiology and fundamental Christian truth means that three main criteria must be used to judge any ecumenism:

1. There must be a common understanding of what is a Christian

Salvation is by grace through faith in Christ. We have already indicated that this Reformation principle has a negative and positive perspective. It means that salvation is not received through human effort or religious rite. Rather salvation is entirely the gift of God, which is received by faith in the completed work of Christ.

2. This understanding must be the basis for an understanding of the church

We have already said that we believe only true believers can make up the church. Other aspects of church life like the sacraments, scripture and authority are vitally important - but they do not define a church. Evangelicals cannot work with what are called 'churches' if they are not truly the church.

3. Any discussion with 'church' bodies who do not agree with this perspective can only be at best discussion and dialogue, but NOT a commitment to a process of unity

There is nothing harmful about discussion; nor, in my view, if positions are made clear need there be any implied guilt by association. Evangelicals will continue to have an important contribution to dialogue between and across denominations. However, the present process is described as a 'commitment' to a process of unity, whose destination is largely undefined. Such a commitment for some Evangelicals, it must be said, already goes too far.

ANDREW GREEN

TOWARDS AN EVANGELICAL THEOLOGY OF ECUMENISM (2)

After long discussion, this paper emerged from the former Advisory Committee for Church Relations, now the Faith and Unity Executive. The paper led, indirectly, to the convening of the Fairmile Twelve, not least to test some of its convictions with some of those known to have reservations about the whole Inter Church Process.

The Baptist Assembly held at Leicester in April 1989 agreed to a continuing involvement in the ecumenical process through the new structures to be known as Churches Together in England (CTE) and the Council of Churches for Britain and Ireland (CCBI). The debate revealed the tensions within the denomination about such ecumenical commitment. Not only did 27% of the representatives present vote against such a commitment, but the views of those voting in favour ranged from the deeply committed to the still faintly suspicious. We ought not to be surprised that such differing views are held sincerely and passionately by those who belong to the churches of our Union. Two words which are characteristic of our life together in Christ are diversity and association. Our roots developed in different soils - Particular and General Baptist, Calvinist and Arminian, for example. Within those differences, however, there is tolerance. We may differ from our brothers and sisters in Christ, but we differ in love. Though we place high value on the local church and its liberty, under the guidance of the Holy Spirit, to administer and interpret the laws of Christ, we believe that our associating together as Baptists, with our differing insights, enhances our witness to the gospel.

FIVE PRINCIPLES

Across our differences we hold fast to the Lordship of Christ in his Church and in the supremacy of Scripture. This concern that we remain faithful to Christ and to the revelation of God through the Scriptures undergirds our commitment to the ecumenical vision. That vision rests upon such scriptural principles as these:

1 **THE UNITY OF GOD:** God has made himself known as Father, Son and Holy Spirit, yet within that diversity remains One.

2 **THE PURPOSE OF JESUS:** The unity of the church is essential for the purpose of Jesus to be achieved, that the world may believe.

3 **THE GIFT OF THE SPIRIT:** Paul asserts that the unity of the church is bestowed by the Spirit.

4 **THE AUTHENTICITY OF LOVE:** Love for God and neighbour are the twin pillars of discipleship. John insists on love of others as an essential criterion against which our love for God must be measured.

5 **THE CHALLENGE OF SOCIETY:** We proclaim reconciliation to God and each other through Christ; such reconciliation must be one of the hallmarks of authentic Christian living.

THE SCRIPTURES

These principles rest - we judge - upon the following passages of Scripture, among others: Matthew 28:16-20; Mark 9:38-41; Luke 6:32-36; 43-45; John 13:34-35; 17:3, 21-23; Acts 2:1-13; 1 Corinthians 3:1-9; 13:1-7; Galatians 3:26-9; 4:7; Ephesians 1:3-10; 2:11-22; 4:1-32; Phillipians 2:1-11; Colossians 1:15-23; Titus 2:11-14; Hebrews 12:14; James 1:19-27; 1 John 3:11-24; Revelation 7:9-12.

TEN THESES

Such an understanding of the Gospel leads us to suggest the following theses. We hope these may prove a bridge upon which all of us in the Baptist family might meet to pray, discuss, agree, and also, in love, diasagree.

1 God is one in three persons. The church must evidence that same unity amidst its diversity.

2 Christ is not divided; neither must the church be.

3   Unity is grounded in our common experience of the cross of Christ and the gift of the Holy Spirit.

4   Unity must manifest itself in positive relations between churches.

5   A divided church cannot with integrity proclaim peace to a divided world.

6   The way of love demands openness and acceptance across human boundaries.

7   Prejudices that have hardened into principles lead to broken relationships.

8   Recognising the presence of the Spirit in others will lead towards healed relationships.

9   To be one in Christ is far more than rejoicing in the fellowship of the like-minded.

10   Unity in Christ is Heaven anticipated.

IMPLICATIONS

To accept such principles and theses has inevitable consequences for our common life in terms of denominational policy towards Churches Together in England (CTE) and the Council of Churches for Britain and Ireland (CCBI); for Association life; for denominational strategy, e.g., sensitivity in church planting and our response to the new Europe; for each local church; and for those many Baptists already involved in local ecumenical projects of various kinds. These implications need to be worked out by us all in the Britain of the 1990s.

INTRODUCTION

During Advent 1991, at the invitation of the Baptist Union's Advisory Committee on Church Relations (ACCR) - which has since evolved into the Faith and Unity Executive - twelve Baptists met at Fairmile Court, Cobham, Surrey. Six of those invited represented those broadly supportive of the 'Yes' vote on the Inter Church Process (ICP) at the Baptist Assembly at Leicester in 1989. They were Faith Bowers, John Briggs, David Coffey, Trevor Hubbard, Douglas McBain and Michael Bochenski. The other six were known to have serious reservations about the ICP and to prefer a 'No' vote. They were Robert Amess, Adrian Argile, Alan Bailyes, John Balchin, Andrew Green and Neil Walker. This was, however, a consultation geared to looking not backwards but forwards.

The then ACCR was increasingly aware that, after the Leicester vote, there had been something of a vacuum in the debate between the YES and NO positions within the Baptist family. It was almost as if the Union had breathed a sigh of relief and said "Thank goodness that's over, now let us get on with it". Several of us had argued against the complacency of that attitude. Partly, of course, this was because we could see the vacuum being filled by - in our judgement - inaccurate and highly provocative literature. Partly also because many of us knew that among the No lobby were people, fellow Evanglicals, whom we both respected and loved in Christ. Those who felt, furthermore, that their voice was not being properly heard in the ongoing debate and who were also concerned about some of the ways that the N lobby was developing within our Union. Not all the unease was one way. Others among us were similarly troubled by, as we saw it, the hijacking and monopolising of the treasured label 'Evangelical' by some within the No lobby. We wished to affirm strongly that it was possible to be a Baptist Evangelical and say Yes with integrity to the Churches Together Movement.

And so we met. To pray, relax, think, listen; to hear and discuss papers; to reinforce our ongoing commitment to the Union and, not least, to its new leadership during this the Decade of Evangelism and of the Listening Process, Towards 2000. It was perhaps a heavenly co-incidence and reminder to us all to discover that at Fairmile, at the same time, were many of the key Restorationist leaders of Britain. A nudge at least, if such were needed, to remember the broader dimensions to Baptist ecumenism in the Britain of the 1990s.

One of the concerns that emerged in the whole process was unease at the poor level of debate and mutual listening that had been achieved in the pre-Leicester Assembly Debate and, indeed, during it. The Fairmile papers were generally well received and suggested to those of us present that bridge-building and points of agreement were indeed possible between us. These papers, rewritten for publication, are now shared with the wider Baptist family in the hope that something at least of the bridge-building that occurred at the Fairmile consultation might be communicated. Above all, these papers are presented in the hope that, during the reviews and ongoing debate of the 1990s, a higher level of listening, discussion and, yes, love might be found among the Baptist family on these so important issues.

The result is this book you are now reading.

MICHAEL BOCHENSKI
Editor
St Albans, March 1993

BAPTISTS AND OTHER CHRISTIANS
An Historical Perspective

REFORMATION SEPARATION

For many centuries the Roman Catholic Church was *the* Church in Western Europe. If we believe the Spirit is continuously at work in the witness of the church, we must recognize that the Spirit's witness was heard through the Roman Catholic Church for much of the Middle Ages. Some Protestant historians have sought an alternative apostolic heritage in radical Christianity, but we cannot escape the fact that the Roman Catholic Church did great things and produced some saintly Christians. By the late Middle Ages, however, it was not in a healthy condition. Its leadership had become too involved in politics, too involved with the secular state; its membership was too inclusive - always a hazard for churches with a parish system; its structures had set too great a distance between priest and people, and between people and God; it was riddled with corrupt practices, like the selling of indulgences; and it was too cumbersome to adapt quickly and so failed to meet people's spiritual needs in an age of change. And the world was changing rapidly. Explorers were pushing out the bounds of the earth; Renaissance scholars were rediscovering the glories of earlier civilisations; the printing press ushered in a new age of communication; and vernacular translations of the Scriptures enabled more people to read the Bible with fresh insight.

The first magisterial phase of the Reformation, defined by the Peace of Augsburg in 1555, won for rulers the right to determine the creed to be adopted within their territory. A later, more radical, phase introduced a new sense of *personal* religion, championing the rights of individual conscience, declaring that one enters the Kingdom by personal response in faith to the grace of God. Key Reformation elements were direct access to God (and hence anti-clericalism), appeal to Scripture, and the nature of authority in the church. Lutheran, Presbyterian and Reformed Churches all stem from this Reformation ferment. Baptists, their parentage more mixed, were among the radicals of the Reformation. In England, the break with Rome was an act of state, less cruel and less fanatical than on the continent. Even so, Anglican Puritans were not all happy about Henry VIII's compromise and eventually many separated. The Independents (Congregationalists) developed from such separation, especially after the Great Ejection of 1662. Among those favouring a *gathered church of believers*, some took a further radical step and became Baptists. The dissenters disagreed with Anglicans on matters of order, discipline and doctrine.

Anglicans tried to enforce uniformity, at times resorting to persecution. During the 1680s two ways of dealing with dissenters were canvassed, called respectively *comprehension* and *toleration*. Comprehension was, in a sense, the ecumenical option: so to extend the basis of the Church of England that only the most obdurate sectarians would remain aloof. This was the preferred option of many, but the High Church Party fought tooth and nail to get it rejected. Toleration, the alternative, back-fired on them, because the toleration of tender consciences necessarily involved the toleration of those without conscience, so that the internal discipline of the Church of England became unenforceable after 1689. The circumstances of leaving the Church of England left bitter memories and even after the Act of Toleration (1689), dissenters continued to suffer religious and civil disabilities.

Meanwhile a counter-reformation brought changes to the Roman Catholic Church, which shed some of its medieval practices. In Britain, Roman Catholics, not conforming to the Church of England, suffered even more severe persecution and disabilities than Protestant dissenters.

Baptists were among those radicals who wanted a 'Believers' Church' - quite diferent from Zwingli's 'Everybody's Church'. This definition, that a church is brought into being by the conversion of individuals, rather than by the proper ministry of Word and Sacrament, is part of our heritage. There is inevitably a big divide between state churches (often more oppressive in their Lutheran than their Anglican form) and gathered churches. This stress and the separation experience encouraged Baptists to form exclusive local fellowships. Associating with other Baptists has not always been easy for churches fiercely protective of their independence under Christ, and relations with other kinds of Christian have been considerably more delicate. Nevertheless, early Baptists often found common cause with other dissenters, especially in the pressure for civil rights. They joined Presbyterians and Independents in the formal organisation of the three denominations from the early eighteenth century. A few early Baptist churches went further in their recognition of other Christians, practising an open table and open membership, in spite of differences over baptism, treating 'saints as saints'. The criterion was still personal faith. The classic statement of the open communion/open membership position is John Bunyan's *Water Baptism No Bar To Communion*.

This brief summary covers many years of tension and strife, which left Baptists strongly anti-Catholic and anti-Anglican, but generally on better terms with Presbyterians and Independents, although not always with other radical groups, especially the Quakers. Such generalisations must be qualified. At an individual level there were good friendships between godly people and it was possible to find Baptists and Anglicans who were openly brothers in Christ.

THE EVANGELICAL REVIVAL

The Evangelical Revival in the later eighteenth century stirred first among the Wesleys and their followers, and among Evangelical Calvinists like George Whitfield and Jonathan Edwards. Baptists were slow to respond to the new mood but eventually they did, led by Andrew Fuller, William Carey and their colleagues in the Northamptonshire Association of Particular Baptists, and by Dan Taylor with the New Connexion of General Baptists. The shared stress on evangelism was an important factor in developing closer relations between the two groups. From the late 1780s, as Evangelicals became dominant in the main churches of dissent and found much in common with Evangelicals in the Church of England, they began to work together, forming various pan-evangelical societies, such as the Sunday School Union, tackling social abuses, like the slave trade, and joining in evangelistic outreach, as in Theatre Services.

As Christians worked more closely together, some felt the need to meet at the communion table. As early as 1790, Robert Hall told the church at Broadmead, Bristol, that he would not be prepared to rebaptize by immersion someone who had been sprinkled *as a believer*. In 1820, speaking to the Anglican National Society (quite remarkable in itself) he claimed, 'Even Catholics and Protestants, influenced by a kindred spirit, can now cordially embrace each other'. He agreed that 'the union of Christians in the promotion of a common cause' was one of the most propitious signs of the times. 'Is it possible', he asked, 'after mixing thus with their counsels, their efforts, their prayers and standing side by side in the thickest of the conflict . . . for them to turn their backs on each other and refuse to unite at the table which is covered with the memorials of his love and the print of his victory?' Unity in mission was the pure gift of God that logically demanded unity at the table. Nobody, he argued, 'is entitled to prescribe as an indispensable condition of communion, what the New Testament has not enjoined as a condition of Salvation'. His debate with

Joseph Kinghorn, champion of the closed table, occupied the years 1815-28, by which time Anglicans and Nonconformists were already pulling away into separate causes. An example of the breakdown of pan-evangelicalism is the virtual withdrawal of Baptist support from the British and Foreign Bible Society because the bishops on the committee would not allow *baptizo* to be translated into Indian languages with any word meaning 'immerse'. Baptists set up their own Bible Translation Society in 1840.

In 1846 some 800 Protestant Christians from Europe and North America met in London to form the Evangelical Alliance, 'the first society formed with a definite view to Christian Unity' (Stephen Neill). Meanwhile a new catholicism appeared. Dissenters were not at all happy about the rise of Anglo-Catholics, although theirs was in its own way a renewal movement. Dissenting attacks on this and on the Establishment of the Church of England were often conducted in the full light of the public eye. At the same time, Nonconformists gradually rid themselves of the earlier civil restrictions, attaining respectability and, for a while, considerable power.

TWENTIETH-CENTURY ECUMENICAL DEVELOPMENTS

The twentieth century has seen a new movement of the Spirit for unity, which was already detectable before the general decline in church-going began to colour the picture. The late Victorian years saw various Methodist groups drawing together, when the effect of irrelevant and sometimes incomprehensible divisions in the churches of Europe and America were impeding effective missionary endeavour. 1891 saw the union of non-Calvinistic Baptists with most of the Calvinistic Baptists. The National Free Church Council was formed in 1893. In 1910, the World Missionary Conference in Edinburgh drew wide support and proved a catalyst for inter-church relations. Baptists took part in this and in subsequent Missionary Conferences. The ecumenical movement, which originated out of this concern for mission, also developed movements for Faith and Order and for Life and Work. Baptists have never been of one mind on ecumenism, but there has been British Baptist involvement in such movements at most stages.

The 1920 Lambeth Conference introduced a new spirit of cordiality and mutual recognition between Anglicans and Free Churches, even though the 'Appeal to all Christian people' to consider organic unity did not seem to Baptists the right way forward. Like the Tractarian movement of the previous century, it made Baptists re-examine their own churchmanship. The Baptist reply focused on the nature of the church, of priesthood and ministry, authority, baptism and the Lord's supper. The kind of union suggested by the bishops was not possible for Baptists, who believed further progress could only be made by 'unreserved mutual recognition'. They were, however, prepared to explore the possibility of *'a federation of equal and autonomous churches in which the several parts of the Church of Christ would co-operate in bringing before men the will and the claims of our Lord'*. This position was reiterated in 1938. Such a body of equal and autonomous churches materialised in 1942 as the British Council of Churches, two years after the Free Church Federal Council had brought together the two earlier Free Church bodies. The BU General Secretary, M. E. Aubrey, was one of the committee of fourteen that drafted the constitution of the World Council of Churches, founded in 1948 as a forum for discussion, communication and joint witness. British Baptists and some other Baptist Unions joined the WCC, but the influential Southern Baptist Convention did not. Many Baptists have remained uneasy about the World Council, concerned about the nature of some participating churches, the bogey of the creation of a 'super church' and controversial social programmes. In 1961 the International Missionary Council was integrated with the WCC.

Churches which practise believer's baptism are never confortable bedfellows for paedobaptists. Our congregational policy means that the Baptist Union cannot speak authoritatively for its member churches in the way of other denominational headquarters, and this complicates our role in such councils. In view of relative size, the Baptist contribution has been remarkably strong in the ecumenical scene, and other denominations usually respect our position, even when they find it hard to understand. In this country the churches have worked together more and more, both at local and national levels, although attitudes to this are inevitably coloured by individual experience, good or bad. On the whole there is more mutual respect nowadays. A mobile population means that churches are much less self-contained, and people's loyalty is less strongly to a particular denomination. The British Faith and Order Conference, held at Nottingham in 1964, looked for great developments by Easter 1980. Anglicans and Methodists looked long and hard at unity proposals. Congregationalists and Presbyterians, later joined by the Churches of Christ, came together in the United Reformed Church. At the local level Baptists have been party to a number of covenanting groups of churches and have joined in various local ecumenical projects (LEPs). The Baptist Union has not given easy assent to ecumenical moves - it was unwilling, for example, to go ahead with the 'Ten

Propositions', and the response to *Baptism, Eucharist and Ministry* made some clear criticisms. When it seemed time for the British Council of Churches to consider radical change, Baptists felt able to participate in the Inter-Church Process, liking the attempt to look for less hierarchy and work more 'from the bottom up'. Again Baptist views affected the final recommendations. Baptists have also been pleased to see Free Church participation widened, especially among the Pentecostal and Black-led churches.

Baptists occupy a bridge position between mainstream denominationalism and the house churches and charismatic groupings of more recent development, and this may be helpful within Churches Together in England, as well as being apparent in other forums which bring churches together, even if they do not use the term ecumenical. Baptists are active in the Evangelical Alliance, the Believers' Church Conference, the Lausanne Movement, etc.

The other major factor in recent developments has been the dramatic change in the attitude of the Roman Catholic Church since the Second Vatican Council. This has been particularly marked in England. It has been remarkable to see Roman Catholics in this country wanting to work alongside those from other churches, even if for many it has been a stumbling block. Baptists have valid questions about the new partnership and our history can inform us helpfully about where we stand and why, but it is irresponsible to make glib assumptions about any Christian groups, ourselves included, based on what they were like three or four hundred years ago.

Our stress on the believers' church, and on the independence under Christ of the local community of believers, will always make us the awkward brigade in inter-church relations, even if we increasingly represent a wider range of baptistic churches. We need to be truly convinced of these principles if we are to make a stand on them. We - and our ecumenical partners - bear with and rise above the problems they present only if we believe that joint effort is more effective in mission. The key question now is:

Faced with the unchurched world, do we now proclaim the Gospel better together?

FAITH BOWERS

A PRAGMATIC WAY FORWARD

In this article, which is really a discussion document, I will postulate various scenarios and suggest ways in which they could be addressed, Please understand that this is an exercise of thinking in print and is not to be considered as either an accurate analysis of the present situation nor as the solution to all our problems.

HANDLING THOSE CHURCHES WHO ARE MAKING THE ECUMENICAL DEBATE AN OPPORTUNITY FOR LEAVING THE UNION

It must be accepted that for many differing reasons there will always be some churches who are unhappy with being linked, however tenuously, to the Baptist Union. Some have inherited an historic affiliation with which they feel no empathy. Others, who feel disinclined to play a financial part in the operations of the Union, consider their continuing membership to be an embarassment. It has to be accepted that some churches, carrying a heavy missionary responsibility, are fully, if not over, committed to the meeting of heavy commitments. The feeling of collective guilt engendered by inability to meet target quotas to the BU Home Mission Fund and Baptist Missionary Society can lead to a parting of the ways. Such churches are also a continuing frustration to Assocation treasurers vainly seeking to meet their targets. These same faithful men and women often unavoidably feel pressurised, and so negative, to those non-contributing churches. The relationships that result from such pressures can sometimes lead to the resolve on the part of the church to separate from the Union.

Some churches feel that the way the local church has developed in its own theological understanding over the years makes the Union at best an uneasy bedfellow and so they desire to cohabit no more! Sometimes, as in the Christological dispute of the early 70's or the ecumenical debate of today, a church can feel on a matter of conscience that a parting of the ways must be engendered. It must be accepted that, with some churches, if it had not been the ecumenical issue, it would have been another that would have prompted their decision to resign from the Union. One says this with no sense of rancour - that is the simple truth. Why is this? Several suggestions can be made.

1. *Leadership* Many, if not most, churches are open to the influence of a strong minister or dominant collective leadership (elders and/or deacons). When the respected leadership of a fellowship over a period of time questions the place of the church in the structures of the Union and Association, then almost inevitably in time there will come a parting of the ways. The given reason might be theological or sociological, but whatever, even though that parting be protracted and painful, the outcome is almost certain. Within the legal framework of the Union there is little that can be done to avoid churches resigning, especially where the denomination is neither a trustee of the building nor holds the deeds of the church, and where the deeds of the church do not specify continuing membership of the Union.

There will always be those leaving the Union for other reasons too, such as:

2. *Separation* In some churches regular teaching is given in such areas as 'guilt by association', 'second degree separation', and the like. Quite obviously, the opportunity of giving another view is never afforded.

3. *Reformed theology and influences* Ministers' conferences are held, widely influential and largely negative to the Union. Other legitimate groupings, such as the Grace Baptist Churches, the Federation of Independent Evangelical Churches or the British Evangelical Council, are perceived as more natural homes for some churches than the Baptist Union.

4. *'Restoration' type influences* Though not so frequently now, there are still some churches seeking 'shepherding' and oversight from one of several charismatic groupings, and they are likely subsequently to feel that affiliation to the Union is no longer appropriate.

5. *Other!* e.g., I can imagine a scenario where, if the Baptist Union continues to become more overtly Evangelical, then some might secede to a more liberal and/or specifically ecumenical environment.

What can the Union do to avoid seepage from membership for the reasons described? Here are a few suggestions:

* A positive initiative in training both ordained and lay leadership as to the biblical principles of association. To seek to demonstrate from the New Testament that mutual responsibility for, and identification with, the wider church family, is a scriptural principle.

* To raise what may be called the ethical implications of a minister taking pastoral charge of a church with a view to changing its constitution and affiliation. If one is prepared to accept the pastorate of a Union-affiliated church in the first place, should not the question be asked as to the ethics and appropriateness of using one's influence to sever that connection other than for exceptional reasons? When I accepted the pastorate of a church affiliated to a Strict Baptist Association, not only did we maintain those links without my becoming a Strict Baptist, but I did as much as I could to make our contribution constructive and meaningful. That seems to me to be only just.

* To seek to demonstrate (I do not know how) that churches that have already taken this route of resignation from the Union have not necessarily been dramatically forwarded in their witness. In fact, possibly, the reverse.

* To explain what is still not always understood: that the Union does not direct the internal actions of a local church, never has and never will. Many congregations leaving the Union either do not understand or it is not explained that the Union upholds and defends the autonomy of the local church.

Nevertheless, given all the above, we must again accept that there will be churches, for whatever reason, who will seek to separate from the Baptist Union, using ecumenism amongst others as the reason, and that very little can be done to stop them.

HANDLING THOSE CHURCHES AT PRESENT COMMITTED TO THE UNION, BUT WHO CONTINUE TO SHOW GENUINE CONCERNS ABOUT ITS ECUMENICAL STANCE.

First, we must concede that there is a *real* problem. To ignore it and hope that it will go away can only be counter-productive in the long term. Then, having registered that this is a serious enough concern for many churches (including some of the most significant in our denomination) to take the decision to opt out of the whole ecumenical process, *we* must now take the initiative to these churches rather than vice versa. Next, there needs to be a discernment, resolve and sensitivity in ascertaining the way ahead. While accepting that one section of the churches cannot control the future agenda for all others, nevertheless consultation and communication are ever the ways for the establishing of confidence. Once a way forward in the ecumenical debate has been arrived at, 'negative' ministers and elders will need to be assured that their integrity is recognised, encouraged as to their continuing role in the denomination, and lastly be educated as to the issues. Will it be affirmed that some of those who have expressed hesitancy in these areas will still be appointed to positions of influence within the denomination? So often ignorance and misunderstanding are the cause of dis-ease and mistrust. It seems to me that very few accredited ministers at the bottom line covet independency and separatism. The Union must come through such ministers as I have described to their churches.

Approaching those churches and leaders who are fully committed to the ecumenical process.

May I, as one who is seriously hesitant where the new ecumenical initiatives and processes are concerned, make a plea for understanding and sometimes restraint by those genuinely committed - for the good of the whole body? Sometimes one gets the feeling that there is no issue that would make some hesitant and that theirs is a commitment come what may. Let both sides of the debate listen to what each is saying and evaluate the points that are made. Especially on those public and publicised occasions when the Union's officers and leaders represent us at ecumenical events, could they please endeavour not to be needlessly provocative to those who, whether from genuine concern or prejudice, are troubled? When actions are taken in all good faith, one photograph or (? mis-)reported utterance can have long-term negative repercussions for the Union. Obviously, if fearful of every reaction, no-one could do anything. Nevertheless, foresight can sometimes mitigate against negativism, especially among our lay people, who do not always understand the issues.

Great care also needs to be taken in the signing of covenants, entering ecumenical projects etc., on the implied assumption that everyone in the Baptist constituency and family are in agreement with, or wish to be identified with, the proposed action. Even when an Area Superintendent is representing only the committed, this is not always understood, nor can it be, without assurances being given. All of that said, I would also want to register here my acknowledgement that those here described as being fully committed to the ecumenical process are also people of conviction, not compromise, who take the action they do in accordance with the light they have received. That was not meant to be as condescending as it sounds!

COMMENTS AND SUGGESTIONS

1. We must accept within a Union of Churches which is 80% Evangelical (if a recent MARC Census is to be believed) **there is a vital necessity for these matters to be handled biblically.** The Roman Catholic issue for many is the main issue and is not just a prejudice inherited from a previous generation. We all know converted priests and Roman Catholic churches that are charismatically aware. But, in the gut of the average Baptist member, there is still (and perhaps rightly) an instinct that wonders whether in truth we are 'Pilgrims Together' or about the same thing when we speak of evangelism with Roman Catholic involvement. Theological pluralism cannot be a satisfactory way forward for anyone. Are any of the issues that caused the Reformation any less issues today? Added to which some of the pronouncements of the Roman Catholic Church since then, and particularly in the last century, have added to these difficulties, not lessened them. It seems to me that Rome today is less flexible than it was. We thank God for renewed biblical awareness and interest in some priests and congregations and would seek to further that, but has the public stance of the Vatican changed? In the context of my own pastorate at Duke Street, Richmond, with an intelligent, theologically articulate congregation, a false or hasty move in this area could blow the church apart. Is it worth it?

2. Again, that said, **I am also anxious lest our denomination be marginalised.** I, for one, want us to be there with the other main-line denominations, both in friendship, growing mutual understanding and the positive seeking for a legitimate visible unity. Yet if we are to be part of that process, there needs must be constant biblical warrant, the preparedness to say NO when a situation demands, absolute openness, and a constant self-examination of motives on the part of the leadership of the Union and its representatives.

3.   **The absolute necessity of ensuring trusted leadership for those
negative to the ecumenical process.** A recognised and respected leader (or
leaders) needs prayerfully to exercise the costly ministry of representing
worried churches and ministers. It is essential, not just that their viewpoint
be expressed, but that it is seen and felt to be expressed.

4.   Because of the long term implications of this debate to the future well-
being of the denomination, **the appointment of, for example, someone of
Area Superintendent-type seniority is needed.**   Even an Area
Superintendent without portfolio, perhaps, but someone who can get
alongside, encourage and represent fearful fellowships. If the concerned
constituency knew that their position was both being understood and
explained, I feel this would be a major step towards dealing with these
concerns.

5.   The need, before this matter is again brought to the Union Assembly in
1995 for a minute **study of procedures as to debate, representation and
voting.** There is a real need to pre-empt the sort of criticism and voting
figure analysis that was entered into after Leicester 1989. Some of the
figures quoted have confirmed fears and concerns. It will not quite do to
speak of the leading of the Spirit in the debate when, as with one church
known to me, a special church meeting was called to discuss its position and
unanimously resolved a certain course of action to its delegates, who then
abstained in the vote.   Where was the guiding Holy Spirit actually
experienced, it must be asked? If we are a Union of *churches* rather than
of *delegates*, that should not happen. Of course such a vitally important
issue only presents itself once a decade to the Assembly. Normally we in
Duke Street would never stipulate voting patterns to our delegates, but this
is that one-in-a-decade issue. The churches will have to know that they have
been heard.

As to voting procedures, when the debate actually takes place I am
hesitant to make suggestions. No immediate solution seems to present itself.
A referendum of the churches would lead to acute problems as to the
wording of the motion and there would need to be some assurance that the
matter had been discussed fairly and voted on properly in the church
meetings. Many of our churches did not even raise the matter in church
meetings prior to the Leicester debate because it was felt either that the
church would not understand the issues or that the debate would be

contentious. With the prior warning as to the timing of the debate, and the airing that the whole matter will by then have received, I tend to favour that the matter should be settled by Assembly, *but on a mandated vote from the churches.* I know that some churches are poor and that others are small, yet on a matter of this importance for all our futures, the decision should be made by those churches who have made the effort and sacrifice involved to be present.

6.   **No Opting Out.** We must do all within our power to avoid the direction which the Anglicans seem to be reluctantly taking over the women's ordination issue. The present 'opting out' provision must never be allowed to have the effect of forming a two-tier Union, such as appears to be envisaged by some within the Church of England.

7.   **The need to grasp the equally painful nettle that some charismatic developments, such as the Summer 1991 Brighton Charismatic Conference, may bring some of the same pressures that we face at the moment from a completely different direction.** A common experience of the Spirit does not cause some of the age-old issues to evaporate overnight. There is much need for work amongst our constituency moving rapidly in a 'Restoration'-type direction. This, too, could lead to an ignoring of issues concerning 'Renewal' that are similarly a problem to some of us.

8.   **The need for trust to grow in the whole gambit of Union life.** That is to say, we all need to have increasingly confirmed, as I believe to be the case, that there is a biblical foundation and a committed Evangelical basis (and not Separatistic) for the Union's activity.

9.   And finally. **May I plead that this process of consultation should not be seen only as an exercise in damage limitation. With the good will of all the interested parties I hope that we will emerge from this process with our understanding of each other enhanced, our ability to work with each other increased and our place as Baptists in the wider ecumenical scene secured.   Then we will be enabled to make that distinctive contribution as Evangelicals and as Baptists which the wider church needs to hear, and also in our turn, to learn from traditions not our own that which will be to our benefit.**

ROBERT AMESS

WORTHY OF TRUST

INTRODUCTION

From our earliest beginnings there is evidence of a profound ecumenical interest among our Baptist forbears. Not surprisingly this has usuallly involved much debate and profound, and on occasions personally costly, disagreement. In this sense there is nothing new to our current discussions. What I hope to show, however, is that today we are not the inheritors of a tradition of theological compromise over this issue that should cause us to apporoach it with inevitable suspicion bordering on alarm. Rather, the truth is that our early history and our recent experiences should combine in enabling us to approach the current round of discussions with more positive and fearless aspirations. I do not profess to know what the future may hold for all of us who are Pilgrims Together. I do believe in the ultimate victory of truth and of Christ over all. So, we should see our participation with other believers in Christ as an opportunity for personal growth in Christ through learning from others, for enriching our spirituality through worshipping with others, and for developing our influence through sharing our own Evangelical heritage and convictions with others who are as open with us as we are with them. I do not believe that this sharing in trust will lead to the diminution of our convictions; nor do I believe that it will lead to a unified Super Church - neither do I hold that such a development would be a desirable end for us even if it were attainable.   But whatever our destiny may be, I do not see that we will find it without reference to our contemporary Christian colleagues who share our struggles with all their joys and pain.

OUR EARLY TRADITIONS

Let us begin by taking three examples from our history which set the scene for our interest in ecumenism.

Thomas Helwys   As a primary pioneer for the underlying philosophy I propose Helwys, the author of the famous plea for all forms of religious toleration.   The historic statement comes in his book, *A Short Declaration of the Mistery of Iniquity*, published in 1612 and dedicated to King James 1. Helwys takes a clear conscience view on the evil of persecution of 'heretics,

Turks or whatever', believing, in common with fellow General Baptists, that all men are redeemable in Christ, not just the elect. Although his views led to his own imprisonment, he gave the finest and fullest defence of the principle of religious freedom that England had ever known up to that point. Since all this took place at a time of great religious oppression and bigotry it marked a radical move of the greatest significance. It sowed the seed of respect for the integrity of the viewpoints of others that is seminal to all healthy ecumenical relationships.

William Carey After Helwys, I see William Carey as the willing initiator of ecumenical sharing. It was in 1792 that he published the famous *Enquiry into the obligation of Christians to use means for the conversion of the heathen* that led to the formation of the Baptist Missionary Society and the beginnings of his work in India. In 1806 he proposed 'the pleasing dream' of a General Association of all Missionary Societies from the four quarters of the world to gather together at the Cape of Good Hope in 1810, at a first meeting for conversation and mutual understanding. Though dismissed as impracticable by his colleague, Andrew Fuller, it is generally agreed that Carey's dream led on much later to the Edinburgh International Missionary Council (1910), from which developed the World Council of Churches. J. R. Nott was the first Chairman of the IMC, having previously led the work of the Student Volunteer Movement whose goal was no less than the evangelising of the whole world in his generation. This evangelical aspiration was a natural development among those whose hearts had first been moved with a vision from Carey.

Shakespeare No, not that one!. For ourselves, however, I see our former General Secretary, *John Howard Shakespeare*, as the suffering prophet for ecumenical involvement, both by the extremism of his views (with which I do not sympathise) and by his tragic death in 1928. Who cannot but feel the personal anguish of his courageous convictions? One incident perhaps shows us something of the cost for him. It took place in Stockholm Cathdedral in July 1923. The cathedral was open to the Baptist World Alliance meeting in that city and Shakespeare was invited to preach. He had chosen as his text Luke 9.62: 'No-one putting his hand to the plough and looking back is fit for service in the Kingdom of God'. Just before his sermon, which was a defence of his own ecumenical pilgrimage, the Bible fell over the edge of the pulpit and crashed to the ground, to the consternation of all there in the cathedral and chiefly to the preacher, who took it as a cruel sign that his life's work was 'done'. Thoroughly unnerved, after the service he began crying uncontrollably like a child. His nervous breakdown was followed by a cerebral haemorrhage in 1925. In his book, *The Churches at the Crossroads*, Shakespeare had argued in favour of episcopacy being taken into our system. He was strongly opposed by T. R. Glover and others, including H. Wheeler Robinson. The Baptist Union of today owes Shakespeare an incalculable debt of gratitude for much of the success of its present structures. In his day, however, he lost the ecumenical argument. Maybe he also lost his life, and certainly his nervous strength, over the issues of ecumenical co-operation which still engage us to this day.

We should not therefore be surprised at the strength of feeling on these issues in the modern debate. There have been many casualties on both sides. We are familiar with the stories of the churches and the pastors that have left us because of their distaste for our involvement and we are the poorer for their departure. There are also the individuals and churches that have paid a great price because of their ecumenical involvement and we should not minimise the cost of that in terms of their lifespan and ministry.

GOALS

At this point, therefore, I enter three preliminary goals for our discussions:

i)   That by honest sharing of our convictions and our questions we can engender some degree of better mutual understanding.

ii)   That we can conduct the debate in a more appropriately Christ-like manner than has often been the case in the past, and without any rancour.

iii) That we accept totally each other's Christian integrity, even when we draw differing conclusions over these matters.

Since J. H. Shakespeare is an influence from our past, this is a very real difficulty. At the time of his major suggestion that we should bring a form of episcopacy into our system, he was charged with pursuing the same loose theological liberalism that Spurgeon had attacked in the days of the Downgrade controversy. If anyone has been used and abused as a hate figure for Baptist demonologists working on a conspiracy theory at the heart of our Union life, then J. H. Shakespeare is that unfortunate one. Yet, if that charge was unfair for him, attacked as he was by some whose theological liberalism was at least as provocative as his own, so today it is just as innacurate to approach the ecumenical issue in a similarly contentious way. Our Union leaders of the past, you see, have NOT sold us down the river!

BEFORE THE INTER CHURCH PROCESS

Allow me to remind you of three significant events in modern times, prior to the Swanwick debate. All of them show conclusively that there never has been and there is not a Baptist conspiracy on these issues. There is a legitimate debate with honestly held differences of viewpoint within it.

1. **The Baptists and Unity Report of 1967**, in response to the Nottingham Faith and Order Conference of 1964. The report was highly significant not only because of its thoroughness but also, and typically, because of its integrity. Thus it highlights the following areas of disagreement: baptism, local autonomy, episcopacy, communion (Lord's supper), creeds and confessions, and church-state relationships. It notes new factors on the modern scene, including the 'new Pentecostalism' that has since become known as charismatic renewal and which is such a potent factor in every facet of the life of our churches today. It draws the conclusion that we need to study more together, consider the issues more, and co-operate better where possible, though with the following caveat: 'It would be a mistake to press the idea of organic union by 1980 lest it endanger denominational unity and thereby seriously weaken the witness Baptists have to make'. *Baptists and Unity* (page 49).

2. **The Ten Propositions** The next phase emerged as a result of the work of the Churches Unity Commission, which proposed to the member churches 'Ten Propositions for Visible Unity'. These propositions, once agreed by all member churches, would have then become the basis for a Covenant of Unity between them to pave the way for even closer integration. With the benefit of hindsight, we now know that the whole process foundered in any event and was therefore abandoned, but what was the approach of the Baptist Union to these discussions? An examination of the facts will again demonstrate the integrity of our response. Dr Morris West wrote the report that was received by the Baptist Union Council and commended to the churches in March 1976. From that source it is plain that:

* We did not agree to abandon so-called 're-baptism' but argued for a proper freedom for Christian judgement.
* We did not agree a Common Ordinal for ordinations in order to satisfy episcopal convictions.
* Indeed, the conclusion Council then reached was as follows: 'It is our clear judgement that at present no clear unqualified recommendation to the Ten Propositions can be made. We have formed this judgement in the light of the provisional responses from our churches and of certain issues elaborated later in this document.'

3. **Baptism, Eucharist and Ministry (BEM)**   The above points surfaced again in our response sent in 1985 to the WCC Faith and Order Paper of 1982, entitled *Baptism, Eucharist and Ministry* (The Lima Text). This was a high-powered consultation among member churches of the World Council of Churches to attempt to summarise the enormous amount of theological convergance that had taken place through decades of honest discussion over these three crucial matters. It sought the response of all who received the Lima Document. Once again, then, the Baptist Union was involved in soundings to the member churches and in responding to the questions which were asked. Did the Union threaten to 'sell the pass' at this stage, or were we well advised on this occasion? Again, a study of the response made in 1982 will reveal the truth of the matter.

Far from betraying our Evangelical heritage, our theological representatives betrayed nothing at all. Accepting many of the valuable insights of the report, especially in the five strands that are woven together to set forth the essential meaning of baptism as participation in Christ's death, conversion, the gift of the Spirit, incorporation into Christ's body, and the sign of the Kingdom, nonetheless they raised weighty criticisms. This can be seen in the following comments from the Baptist Union's official response document of 1985:

> The problem is compounded by what may well be an inevitable feature of ecumenical statements, namely an ambiguity of language allowing formal assent in the teeth of suspected unbridged disagreement.

On baptism, the Lima affirmation was that 'any practice that might be interpreted as re-baptism must be avoided.' To this the BU Council said, 'This statement is wholly unacceptable in its present form since, on some interpretations, nothing could pass through so restrictive a sieve.' In any case, this was more of a study document than anything else. The formal covenant proposals had already collapsed. With others among our colleagues, we could see no easy answers to these complex issues, but we still wanted to participate in discussions, though without surrendering our own deeply held and biblically based Baptist convictions.

SWANWICK AND LEICESTER

In the light of all this hard theological and ecumenical work, conscientiously fulfilled, we come to the *Inter Church Process* and the *Swanwick Declaration* of 4 September 1987, 'No longer Strangers but Pilgrims'. Essentially, this fresh initiative began differently and with a different set of goals. Its beginnings were in an informal gathering for prayer and reflection at Lambeth Palace in 1984. Our then General Secretary, Bernard Green, was present. There followed many discussions and a whole range of soundings, culminating in the now famous broadcast Lent Course supported by over one million people, entitled *What on earth is the Church for?* The so-called 'Mersey Miracle' of the 1980's, with Anglican, Free Church and Roman Catholic partnership at leadership (and many other) levels was also a formative influence here. This led on to the Swanwick Conference and Declaration of 1987. Beyond that to the famous 'Marigold document' (or the 'yellow peril' as some unaffectionately called it!), with its detailed draft proposals for new ecumenical instruments in our nation/s. Like our own Declaration of Principle, this affirmed a simple credal basis in confession of the Lord Jesus Christ as God and Saviour, according to the Scriptures, with a stress on the Trinity. It called for a commitment to obey God's will, to depend on the Holy Spirit and to search for deeper communion. It emphasised mission and evangelism. It also expressed a desire to become more fully. 'in his own time', one Church united in faith, communion, pastoral care and mission. Unity in diversity was its keynote.

It proposed for England, for example, a simpler structure, with a national Forum every two years, an Enabling Body, a small staff, and two Field Officers. A new body to oversee and co-ordinate inter-church work in the whole of Britain and Ireland was also envisaged. Crucially, too, there was an acceptance that each participating denomination should work within its own authority structures. The decision reached at Leicester in 1989, with the support of nearly 74% of those present, was to our fuller participation as Baptists in just such a pilgrimage and search together. Meticulous consultation and preparation, involving several mailings to each church in the Union, had preceded the eventual debate.   This long and involved process has been difficult for some other church bodies to understand.   For us, however, the combined decision reached at Assembly by each local church who had made both the time and - yes - the money available to be represented, is the only ultimate authority we know as a Union under God. Whilst recognising and respecting a legitimate difference of opinion in our midst, the decision was honourably taken.   Indeed, the Assembly called all participants to 'maintain in their differences a mutual love and trust that accords with their fellowship in Christ'.   It is reasonably clear that the proportions of the vote then were in line with our previous Baptist ecumenical heritage and experience.   The major new factors, however, were the presence and activity of the Roman Catholic Church as a constituent member *and* of some of the new Black-led Churches, together with some Pentecostals.

Since the Leicester Vote, taken in 1989, we have then been critically but constructively involved in Churches Together in England (CTE) and in the Council of Churches for Britain and Ireland (CCBI).

THE PRESENT AND THE FUTURE

Apart from a detailed argument over the Leicester statistics, which is neither fruitful nor well founded in my opinion, some of our friends in a loosely-knit new organisation named FAB (The Fellowship of Anxious Baptist - aren't we all?!) have raised the issues of our participation in the Inter Church Process once more.   It is important to note that at this point FAB is not calling on Baptists to leave the Union over this issue, though sadly, some have done just that.   What they are saying is that they intend to encourage widespread discussion of the issues - which is no bad thing and to which I do not have the slightest objection.   Let the discussion be based on accuracy and truth, however: e.g., it is totally misleading to suggest, as some do, that our commitment to CTE is uniform, uncritical and all embracing.   Or that it is secretly geared to a future 'Great Church' in Britain which is even now in its final stages of coming together.   Perhaps in this regard we are only hearing again the same views that have been expressed in former days by others subscribing to the Union conspiracy theory?   No good thing can ever come, say such in all generations, from this whole ecumenical business.   In the end there will be a sell out to Rome!   And so it goes on . . .

A careful examination of all the facts should be enough to calm these fears. I cannot for one moment believe that our ecumenical colleagues themselves would wish such a notion to succeed or be propagated! They really do appreciate our contribution *as it is*. If the Baptists are there, many say, then at least we can be sure that they have brought with them their Bibles and their theological evangelicalism! Because that is what we are renowned for; *they* will never allow us to depart from it. Nothing in heaven or earth could persuade us to abandon our Evangelicalism anyway.

ON REALITY AND WAYS FORWARD?

What then is a more likely ecumenical scenario in the rest of this exciting decade?

* *LEPs* First at local church level within our Baptist Union family there is no doubt that Local Ecumenical Projects (LEPs) are here to stay. At a recent count for England and Wales 102 of our churches were involved as partners with a variety of other churches, sharings buildings, resources, mission and ministry.

* *Catholicism* It is evident that Catholics are around the evangelical scene these days, even in our mass evangelism. They are openly involved in charismatic renewal and attend Spring Harvest and the like. Many of our most conservative scholars are prepared to express openly their gratitude to the works of their Roman colleagues. There are nowadays excellent Catholic evangelists whose Gospel preaching commands the respect and support of Christians from a wide spectrum of the Church. All of this points to the fact that huge changes have already occurred both within us and also within the Roman Church. Quite apart from our more detailed interpretations of Vatican 2, plainly at the level of mutual perception, things are no longer as they once were. Nor will they ever return to the former animosities and misrepresentations, please God.

* *No surrender!* I see no possibility at all ever of our surrender of believer's baptism in favour of the practice of infant baptism. There is no doubt that other churches are more aware than ever of the ambiguities of their position through the insistence of our own within a mutual acceptance of each other's convictions. The reality is that we too have to face the fact that we are nowhere near as clear-cut in our practice of New Testament

conversion-baptism as our views might often suggest: e.g., in too easy acceptance of profession of faith in open membership churches at the expense of a firmer challenge to baptism. That said, there is diversity in unity here too! There is no way in which we can abandon our convictions regarding the integrity of *each local church governing its own affairs.*

* *Episcopacy* Since the episcopacy argument has been around for us since at least 1919, I cannot see that we are likely to abandon the value of our own ordination and ministry. Or, I hope, Superintendency! T. R. Glover won then and would probably win now! Yet there is little doubt that if the episcopacy sheds its hierarchical and authoritarian presuppositions as the top of a threefold form of ministry (bishop - priest - deacon) - we may then have more to share.

* *No groundless fears* I repeat the observation that we have been painstakingly careful in this debate for the last seventy years. During this time we have as a Union become much more theologically conservative in some respects, though I would hope more radically open in others. At a time when our new General Secretary has purposefully 'Listened to the Family', is it likely that all of a sudden we will abandon care, restraint and thought in order to compromise here over ecumenism? A a time when, in fact, our evangelical zeal is leading us into adventurous plans for church planting, outreach among the minority-people groups and renewed social concern, and when our influence in ecumenical affairs is on the increase, is the myth of 'sell-out' really a likely scenario?

AND FINALLY

My personal expectations lead to different goals which I summarise thus:

1. We should stay firmly in the processes of the CTE and CCBI in order to encourage their shaping - *towards mission.* At times, in my limited experience, our closest allies in the process will be the Romans! For all of us, our profound hope must be that of a Carey or a Mott, in more effectively reaching the greatest number with the Gospel Word.

2. There is more than one form of ecumenism, however, and so we should also reach out to those who are our more obvious allies - the Pentecostals, Brethren, Independent Evangelicals, Strict Baptists and New

Church groupings, some of whom will abhor our other connections, but some of whom will be grateful for them.

3. We should commit ourselves to the production of an Evangelical Theology of Ecumenism which can present a reasoned case for a vigilant but positive involvement by the Baptist Union of Great Britain in Churches Together in England and the Council of Churches for Britain and Ireland in the future. This series of essays is, of course, part of that process itself. None of us knows what that involvement will lead to, but we do know that the present journey will be full of hope, peace and God's own wonderful surprises.

DOUGLAS G. T. McBAIN

UNITY AND TRUTH

In the ecumenical debate there are, fundamentally, two issues which are frequently - and unfortunately - confused:

1. THE ECCLESIOLOGICAL ISSUE

a) **Committed Membership** Our conviction about believer's baptism carries with it an implicit understanding of the nature of the church. This is because, although with other communions we regard baptism as an initiatory rite, we maintain that in New Testament times it was practically synchronous with, and indeed expressive of, personal faith. Baptism, faith and membership of the Body of Christ went together. Consequently, those who practise believer's baptism also require a personally committed church membership. Historically, the baptism of children - even the children of believers - has not only radically altered the rite, it has also altered the conception of the church. The church becomes an inclusive body, comprising believers and (at best) potential believers. In some denominations (e.g., Anglicans and, on the continent, Lutherans) the picture has been confused even further by a Constantinian understanding of the church as a state affair, where all within a particular territory are regarded as notionally Christian and members of the church.

b) **A Union not a Church** The 'gathered' or 'committed' understanding of the church carries with it a further implication regarding its government. The New Testament word 'church' (*ekklesia* - better translated 'assembly') applies to God's people, either universally (the truly 'catholic' church, comprising all God's people, past, present and future, existing both in heaven and on earth), or locally as the empirical expression of that universal reality. The New Testament conception of the headship of Christ must therefore be applied and worked out in local terms for each group of believers. This is fundamental to our congregational understanding of church government. Because of this, however, Baptists have traditionally maintained that the use of the term 'church' to represent a denominational body is unjustified. All such groupings are, in modern parlance, para-church organisations. This applies equally to the Baptist Union, long recognised by Baptists as a voluntary federation of autonomous local churches. Hence there are Baptist churches which are equally 'Baptist' outside the Union, either in other Unions or groupings (e.g., the Federation of Independent Evangelical Churches - FIEC) or entirely independent. This, of course, has implications for our Baptist Assemblies as well as for other denominational structures. We have no real biblical justification for regarding them as a sort of surrogate church meeting. To determine the true mind of the Union, we need to consult individual churches and not just their delegates. The problems with this latter situation are highlighted when delegates choose to vote contrary to the wishes of their churches.

c) **Consensus in diversity** Although there have been times when the position has appeared to be irksome to some who would wish to have made the Union more ecumenically adaptable, in general terms, Baptists right across the theological spectrum have maintained these principles, and resisted attempts to erode them. In the past Baptist leaders, whose preferred theological position was far from conservative, have stoutly defended this understanding of ecclesiology in ecumenical debates, and we must be sincerely grateful to them for that.

2. THE THEOLOGICAL ISSUE

A Historical Diversity. Historically, Christians of all persuasions have insisted that meaningful relationships with other professing believers needed to be tied to what were considered to be the fundamentals of the faith. The historical creeds and confessions (including our own Baptist confessions) bear witness to this fact. Although, with hindsight, we might deplore the theological hair-splitting of the past, we have to admit that there is an essential truth in this assertion. How *can* two walk together unless they are agreed? However, it would be patently naïve - or intellectually dishonest - to maintain that all professing Christians believe the same things. We are deeply divided when it comes to the presuppositions which determine our approaches to the Faith. In the days of the Protestant Reformation, differences had to do with the authority of Scripture and what it taught about the nature of Grace. It was this that undermined Roman Catholic sacramentalism. Whilst it is right and proper to recognise and rejoice in much that has been happening in modern Roman Catholicism, the official position has not fundamentally changed. We should also note that what we see in this country is a very mild form of Romanism. The situation was further complicated, however, with the development of the rationalistic liberalism of the nineteenth century, and now by its modern heirs. This naturalistic approach to the Faith is fundamentally opposed to the supernaturalistic presuppositions assumed in Scripture. Ironically, at this point, the Conservative Evangelical finds he has more in common with the Catholic than with those of 'modernist' persuasions.

Evangelical Unity and Diversity That this is a considerably broader issue than a denominational one is apparent from the way in which Conservative Evangelicals have for many years (and long before the ecumenical movement got under way) happily co-operated across denominational boundaries. The Evangelical Alliance is the classic expression of what has long been regarded as our 'spiritual' (over against our denominational) unity. It is also apparent, however, in a good number of missionary societies and other para-church organisations. In a negative sense, we have seen the principle at work destructively within our Union from Downgrade to the present day. Those who join the Baptist Union have to take on board the fact that they are identifying with a federation of churches which is itself theologically inclusive.

THE PRESENT CRISIS

A crisis of conscience

Until recently, in general terms, the autonomy of the churches within the federation has allowed those with different theological interests to coexist, albeit uneasily at times. More, it has been possible for Baptists to engage to a certain degree in ecumenical co-operation with other professing Christians of different theological persuasions with no crisis of conscience. Issues of common humanitarian or social concern may even unite us in concerted action with non-Christians, let alone with other believers. In practice a 'self-adjusting' situation has obtained, where individual churches have gone as far as they felt they wanted to, depending largely on the local situation.

It has been the more recent ecumenical initiatives which have produced the problems. The invitation to 'commitment' and 'covenant' (whatever those terms might mean) with those holding radically different views, and with what seems to be a pretended ignorance of our intended destination, goes beyond the acceptable limits of conscience and conviction for some of us. A 'unity' which assumes that fundamental differences do not matter, or which is based on a sort of legal fiction that they do not exist, seems to us little short of intellectual dishonesty.

Interpretation

It is not sufficient to maintain that we are quibbling over interpretations of the Faith rather than the Faith itself. It is beyond question that, whatever our theological stance, we all bring our subjective particularity to Scripture. To then argue that, consequently, we can only know truth subjectively, or that objectivity is beyond our grasp and therefore a fallacious pursuit, is unnecessarily pessimistic. It is apparent that the New Testament authors understood truth to be objective (however it might have been subjectively appreciated) and that they insisted on adherence to objective truths when it came to matters of Faith and Order. That is why, for example, even a shared Trinitarian confession is inadequate as a basis for co-operation in that, in the present climate, the Trinity is subject to a range of 'interpretations', some of which are mutually exclusive. In this respect we are far removed from our forbears who laboured over the creeds and confessions we have inherited with a view to defining exactly what they believed and did not believe.

A valid criticism of thinking in ecumenical circles has been that it has attempted to frame 'catch-all' statements which may be accepted by all, but which in practice allows those involved to read into them whatever significance they wish. The assumption, apparently, is that either theological agreement may be minimal - a sort of lowest common denominator - or that theological statements must be studiously ambiguous, thus allowing for the widest range of interpretation. But surely this is an instance of papering over the very real cracks? The fact that we may be using the same words as others and yet be meaning something totally different should cause us concern. Does this approach provide any substantial basis for common action? If, as we are repeatedly assured, the aim of ecumenical co-operation is mission, is this meaningful when we cannot even agree on the message?

Separation

Perhaps it ought not to surprise us that, for some, the current developments have become the reason for their leaving the Union. There is, of course, nothing new in this line of action. Enough of our original Separatist and

Restorationist (in the broad sense) ethos remains to make staying or leaving almost a perennial issue. Where we draw the limits of acceptable orthodoxy has been a problem for us since the time of the English Reformation. There will always be those who insist on certain issues as essential which others regard as incidental. However, we need to consider the fairness of imposing that sort of crisis of conscience on one another. When a minister or a church decides to sever their links with the Union, such a decision is frequently the result of prolonged and agonised heart-searching. It is not necessarily the case that such people are being difficult. It is simply that they cannot square what they see the Union and its leadership doing with their own consciences. It is true that individual churches have been able to opt out of the Churches Together commitment, but we need to realise how such a stance appears to those working in a centralised denominational system. A refusal to get involved with local ecumenical matters gives the impression that we are being unreasonably awkward, when in reality we are only being Baptist! Freedom of conscience with regard to what individuals or churches consider to be non-negotiable truth is a principle on which many of our forbears staked their freedom and sometimes their lives.

CONCLUSION

It seems a pity that, at this time, when many of us have more confidence in our Union leadership and are more optimistic about the possibilities for the Union than ever before, some of us should be placed in the embarrassing and awkward position of having to disagree with them on what is, after all, a national issue. Unless words mean nothing, the basis of Churches Together in England is simply unacceptable to many. The ambition to influence the ecumenical debate from within may be laudable, but on the current terms, a good number of us feel that the price is too high.

JOHN BALCHIN

BAPTISTS AND ROMAN CATHOLICS

Let me begin with a brief piece of autobiography. All my life I have lived with the tension of this divide and tried to bridge it. I do not just believe in bridge-building, I have lived it as the child of a 'mixed' marriage. My father was a Polish Catholic refugee who fled from the murder of his parents and from a Stalinist slave camp to Britain during World War 2. In Nottingham he met and married my mother who came from an East Midland miner's family with Baptist roots going back into the nineteenth century. I grew up with a love and affection for Poland, its people and its church. I also grew up spiritually in a Baptist church a few hundred yards from our home and there it was that I first discerned the fragrance of Christ and later found and followed him.

There are at least three main Baptist approaches to relationships with Roman Catholics and, of course, vice-versa: (i) the Sectarian. (ii) the Bridge-Builder, and (iii) the Evangelist - who is prepared not only to cross the bridge but also to work and co-operate together, at times, in the cause of evangelisation. To illustrate:

The Sectarian

* 'If I could but sink my teeth in Luther's gullet, I would not hesitate then to come to Mass and there drink with bloody mouth.' (A sixteenth-century Catholic)

* 'Romanism is not Christian, but the Devil's masterpiece. The Pope is Satan's Vicar here on earth and the anti-Christ. Have NOTHING to do with Popery. It is the Gospel's greatest enemy and the great persecutor of God's people and is under the curse of Almighty God.' (A twentieth-century Baptist after my 'YES' articles on the 1989 Inter Church Process debate had appeared in the *Baptist Times*)

The Bridge-Builder

* 'I do not deny that I seek peace wherever possible. I believe in listening to both sides with open ears. I love liberty. I will not, I cannot, serve any faction. I have said that all of Luther's teaching cannot be suppressed without suppressing the Gospel but . . . I do not see that I

am called upon to approve everything he has said since.' (Sixteenth-century Catholic reformer, Desiderius Erasmus)

* 'Flee formulae; bear with the weak. While all faith is placed in Christ, the thing is safe. It is not given to all to see the same thing at the same time.' (Sixteenth-century Protestant reformer, Martin Bucer)

The Evangelist

* 'The result of all the efforts to achieve Christian Unity will be inward-looking, preoccupied with our own "Churchy" experiences, unless there is also an outward journey into God's world. The journey Christians are to make together must continue in the context of mission, with a consciousness of God sending us out into the world.' (Sheppard and Worlock).

* 'We can seek to develop a spirit of mutual respect . . . We can renounce our hostility towards one another and we can cut out campaigns of sheep-stealing. We can share in detail our training materials, our methods and techniques, learning from one another what works best in what circumstances . . . Finally we can learn from one another's experiences of using the spiritual gifts. Let us not forget that we want to evangelise with signs and wonders in the power of the Holy Spirit, with miracles and signs following.' (Fr Kevin Ranaghan, speaking at the Brighton Charismatic Consultation in 1991)

ON DISAGREEMENTS AND RESERVATIONS

Most Baptists, including the present author, would have reservations, major and minor, about many aspects of Roman Catholicism. The primacy/cult of the Pope, intercessions to and veneration of saints, the adoration of Mary, the insistence on celibacy, the use of rosaries and Hail Marys, the insistence on (? coerced) confession, the doctrines of the Mass, the number of the biblical sacraments/ordinances (7 versus 2), the claim of papal infallibility (albeit rarely exercised), understandings of grace . . . etc. These are often the meat of discussions, debates, conferences and fraternals wherever Baptists and Roman Catholics do actually meet in friendship to build bridges. It has to be frankly recognised that significant movement, on either side, on these issues is unlikely. Baptists will continue to reject them and the understanding of the Gospel that undergirds them while most Catholics will affirm and defend them. For some Baptists, quite simply, that is the end of the debate. For some the Anabaptist/Catholic position has not changed at all over four centuries and is unlikely to for another four at least, if ever: Maranatha!

ON INTEGRITY, AGREEMENTS, SHARED TRUTHS AND SHARED SAINTS

The key question which divides those who remain proud to be both Evangelicals and Baptists is whether the above differences rule out any partnership at all in the Gospel with Catholics. Let me try to put the questions bluntly from the opposite perspective to my own. Are Catholics Christians at all? Can we co-operate with people who believe such things, even in fulfilling the Great Commission in this Decade? Do not the above practices and beliefs really de-christianize all Roman Catholics from, so to speak, the Pope down? How can Christ dwell within the hearts, lives and churches of people who will not break with such practices and who indeed affirm them? Is the only way to become a 'proper' Christian to leave Rome and join the varied and, yes, fragmented world of Protestants? Again let it be clearly said that our own divisions here are exactly mirrored among the Catholic faithful, many of whom have problems accepting that anyone can be both Protestant and truly Christian. To continue: do we compromise truth just by being in association with Roman Catholics? Of course, there are particular born-again Christians here and there within Catholicism, as is often agreed, but should we be in partnership with its hierarchy and church government structures? Do Catholics, as it were, 'contaminate' us and the integrity of the Gospel we preach by *any* meaningful relationship or partnership with them? 'Come ye apart from them' is the conclusion those who share these concerns reach or, perhaps, simply inherit.

On issues as deeply felt as these it is hard indeed to build bridges, create mutual understanding and encourage even the slightest movement of position. Ah, but with God all things are possible (Luke 18:27). Below I list some of the reasons why some Baptist Evangelicals have felt it possible to support the YES decision at Leicester and the closer co-operation with British Catholics that has flowed from the formation of Churches Together in England and the Council of Churches for Britain and Ireland.

* The often very 'mainstream' interpretation of the Bible - Roman Catholics usually have few doubts about the virgin birth, the deity of Christ or the resurrection, for example! Some affirm these more loyally than fellow Baptists or certain Protestant bishops.

* Many Catholics are also far more respectful of the Bible and of its authority than many Protestants we could name. The publication of the *Jerusalem Bible* in the 1960s after Vatican 2 was a watershed in British Catholicism. Two decades or so later the vernacular Scriptures are continuing to do their blessed work within Catholic churches and homes across Britain. Deo Gloria!

* The Christian Catholic/Protestant moral and religious consensus on, say, world development issues and on sexual and personal morality - on issues like Sunday trading, Third World debt, pornography, homelessness. sexual orientation, family life, and the environment we so often stand better together.

* The unequivocal affirmation by Roman Catholics of the supremacy of Christ over and against, say, Islam, Marxism, Hinduism, Secular Humanism, Materialism and New Ageism.

* Shared hymns, prayers, worship, songs, sanctuaries, cathedrals *and* Scriptures. We were all Catholics once! For well over 1000 years, warts and all, the Catholic Church in the West preserved for us all the Scriptures and the traditions, buildings, great prayers and hymns of the Christian faith. This debt is not acknowledged anywhere near enough by those who prefer to remember only Peter's pence and a diet of worms!

* Christian Roman Catholic/Baptist co-operation and friendship - in chaplaincies (college, hospital, industry), fraternals, community, schools, night shelters, action groups and charities. Our common humanity we find is undergirded by a Christian faith, differently understood at times, but real to us all.

* The Lord's teaching on love - love that accepts and trusts across the boundaries; love that refuses to slander, label, demean. Milk of human kindness love. Good Samaritan love. Love for tax collectors and 'sinners'. Love with risk. John 13 love. Calvary love.

* The good and great Catholics of church history - Augustine, Justin Martyr, Boethius, Benedict, Julian of Norwich, Aquinas, Francis and Clare, Erasmus, St John of the Cross, Thérèse of Lisieux, Loyola, Gerard Manley Hopkins. . . ; and also in our own age - Mother Teresa, Tolkien, G. K. Chesterton, Lech Walesa, Dom Helder Camara, Oscar Romero, Derek Worlock and Malcolm Muggeridge, to name but a few. Can we really deny Christ in - and so de-christianize - all these people who were both pleased and able to stay within Rome?

UNITE AND DIVERSITY - BEWARE STEREOTYPES

Roman Catholicism *has* moved since the days of Luther, despite my *Baptist Times* correspondent's views above! The Catholicism of the Counter-Reformation was often very different from the corrupt and immoral 'Rome' that Luther knew and protested against. Some of it, however, was worse! We must beware generalisation. Contemporary Roman Catholicism too has many faces. It is even more diverse, rich and varied than is our own Baptist family. Too many Baptists speak, condemn and judge Catholicism in ignorance, both of church history and of the twentieth-century world church. More Baptists need to read some of the Roman Catholic writings of the post-war years. Let us look briefly at some examples. In Eastern Europe who can fail to be moved by the Catholicism that inspired Solidarity, e.g., Cardinal Wyszynzki's *A Freedom Within* or the murdered priest Jerzy Popieluszko's moving sermons, *The Price of Love*. The Latin American theologians of liberation and the suffering base communities likewise are revealing a very different kind of Catholicism, and are often paying the price in blood - or expulsion - for those differences. Witness, for example, Jon Sobrino's *The True Church and the Poor*, or the Nicaraguan Baptist/Roman Catholic partnership of Jorge Pixley and Clodovis Boff in *The Bible, the Church and the Poor*. See also Leonardo Boff's fine *Ecclesiogenesis*, which is largely 'Free Church' in both its sympathies and conclusions.

In England, witness the writings of, for example, the late Malcolm Muggeridge or of Derek Worlock or Gerard Hughes. Consider also the excellent (conservative) Catholic Biblical Commentaries - like Schnackenburg on John. Witness too the highly significant role of Catholics in the charismatic movement of the 1970s and 1980s. Acts 10:44-6 captures well the similar amazement this gave rise to at the time among such as David du Plessis and Michael Harper! Cardinal Suenens and Francis Macnutt wrote as Catholics, remember. Witness here the recent Catholic involvment in the Ecumenical Charismatic Consultation on Evangelisation at Brighton in 1991. The Catholic family, like our Baptist one, is varied, complex and diverse. It is, then, spiritually and intellectually dishonest to lump 'Catholicism' together into one huge Aunt Sally and then to fire; or to interpret it still through largely sixteenth-century eyes or glasses.

ON OTHERS' INTEGRITY

Perhaps a key tenet of the law of love in the late twentieth-century Body of Christ is this: beware of robbing others of their integrity before Christ in the process of affirming your own! Helwys revisited? This applies to brother and sister Baptists as well as to our relationships to those people, millions of them, who are Catholics. This point was similarly and powerfully made by Cardinal Newman in his nineteenth-century classic, *Apologia pro vita sua*. It is not an easy read for a Baptist (!), but is a well thought out and well argued defence of his own conversion *to* and not from Rome. This he describes as 'like coming into port after a rough sea'. As he writes in the book: 'We do not find the difficulties which you do in the doctrines that we hold'.

THE INTERNATIONAL DIMENSION

One final observation: the Baptist family worldwide is a large and, of course, an international one. The principle which operates here must surely be that each Baptist Union must relate to the Catholicism prevalent in its own country, whilst being aware at least of the ripple effect! The English Catholicism of, say, a Basil Hume or Derek Worlock and of the Roman Catholic CTE /CCBI representatives some of us have met at the Swanwick Conferences requires, I believe, a Christ-like bridge-building response from Baptists, not least with the mutual urgency of contemporary evangelisation of the vast army of the unchurched in mind. How difficult, though, to explain this British response to the Polish Baptists, a courageous and yet beleaguered minority. They are still sometimes persecuted and often sadly indoctrinated in the belief that a good Pole and a good Catholic are one and the same. The Brazilian Baptists, it would seem, or so some recent mission statistics demonstrate, see all Roman Catholics as potential converts. Let me say that I too have had the privilege of leading lapsed or nominal Catholics to Christ, and some lapsed and nominal Baptists too! Or consider the

Northern Ireland Baptists whom some of us have had the privilege of meeting at Mainstream in recent years. For them to enter into partnership and even relationship with Catholics will have all sorts of implications, from threats to life through to guilt about betraying the victims of sectarian violence or, indeed, their nation. World Catholicism is not uniform and monochrome: nor should be the responses to it of our world's many Baptist Unions, We can only make our own British Baptist response and answer to our Lord for it.

I re-wrote this article in the Baptist Missionary Society Bi-Centenary year. I conclude with this splendid quote from the man who has perhaps been our greatest gift as Baptists to the world church:

> Let us conscientiously profess our own convictions; but let us love but little the man of our sect who possesses little of the image of Christ, whilst we love him exceedingly in whom we see so much of Christ, though some of his opinions are contrary to our own. So shall we know we are passed from death into life and sectarian quarrels will cease. (William Carey).

Amen.

MICHAEL I. BOCHENSKI

THE ANTI-ECUMENICAL
AND PRO-ECUMENICAL MIND

The story is told of the man who, losing himself in a strange city, asked for directions from a passer-by. 'Well, sir', said the stranger, 'you will have to turn left, then right, then over the roundabout . . . in fact it is so complicated, if I were going where you want to go, I wouldn't start from here.' The problem with ecumenism is that we all start in different places! Our temperament, family background, church, and home town - all affect us profoundly. This may be a statement of the obvious, but we need to recognise its importance early in any debate about ecumenical involvement. In any sort of discussion there are often misunderstandings because people with different backgrounds start in different places. In every debate there is the need to clear the ground of misunderstandings and provide a framework of thinking that enables us to talk together using the same language. There is a need to make sure that the words and ideas employed mean the same thing, whatever side of an argument we represent.

In this debate about the ecumenical movement, however, it is not just a question of using the same language, it is a matter of understanding different 'mind sets'. Just as an American or an African will have different perspectives compared with the English mind-set, so the anti-ecumenical mind-set may well be different from the pro-ecumenical mind-set. They may not only speak different languages but also come from different perspectives and with different attitudes. The purpose of this essay is to expose some of the underlying reasons for different mind-sets in the hope that we can then get closer to understanding one another's language and attitudes.

QUESTIONS OF BACKGROUND

1. Personal experience of a wider Christian world

Ecumenical encounter often begins with friendship. It is almost inevitable that we have suspicions of Christians with other 'labels'. When, however, we develop a friendship and then discover a 'born again' believer, this opens the door to re-evaluating where we stand on ecumenical encounter generally. The number of such links and friendships will determine something of our attitude. It frees us of suspicion and opens us to the possibilities we had not imagined before. Those Baptists with a pro-ecumenical mind are likely to be those who have looked for and so had good experiences of friendship across denominational divisions. Those who are of an anti-ecumenical mind are similarly likely to have had bad experiences of such personal encounters. Both groups, however, must ask tough questions of themselves.

Those of pro-ecumenical mind must ask the question, 'How much does my experience of friendship obscure issues of truth?' Because we do not like to hurt people or offend people, we sometimes conveniently neglect areas of doctrinal difference which may be important. Those of an anti-ecumenical mind must ask the question, 'How much do issues of truth bring barriers which love and understanding can overcome?' It is quite possible that we can be so belligerent and uncharitable that we can never see anything good in someone with a different point of view. Witness the 1992 General Election !

b)   Church experience of the wider Christian world?

Good and bad experiences of the ecumenical movement will naturally cloud our present perspective on ecumenism, for example, experiences of joint evangelism, joint social action, joint worship. To these experiences we can add the influence of our reading and the prejudices of our particular theological background. Again, we must ask questions of both positions. Those with a pro-ecumenical mind, with generally good experiences, need to recognise with *realism* some of the problems others have suffered. Mere romanticism about ecumenical involvement will not do! Those with an anti-ecumenical mind, who have bad bad experiences, need to recognise with *hope* some of the experiences of others. Mere pessimism about ecumenical involvement will not do!

2. PYSCHOLOGICAL QUESTIONS

It is clear that our background, temperament and spirituality are closely intertwined and help to make us what we are. There is nothing wrong with this state of affairs, since God made us all gloriously different. If all thought the same, felt the same and did the same, life would be exceedingly dull. This fundamental variety in any family has important implications for the way we perceive issues. Very often our attitudes on spiritual issues have as much to do with our temperament as they do with our theological convictions. Because of this we need to be clear *why* we react in certain ways. Are our motives always right? For example, all of us have a very deep desire to 'belong'. The love and support of a like-minded group is of inestimable pyschological value, but the price tag of belonging is the adoption of the 'group' view. We dare not deviate!   Thus, *fear* of what others think of us may become more important than what the Bible says or than practising love. This may be true for people in any camp.

On the one hand there is a sort of spirituality where you prove your orthodoxy by showing how 'anti' you can be: you show that you belong by what you are against. The particularly unfortunate effect of this attitude is that suspicion is rated as a higher virtue than love. Self-consciousness and the desire to please others becomes more important than self-forgetfulness and the desire to please Christ. On the other hand, there is another sort of spirituality where toleration, acceptance and love are the virtues which are prized above others. In this case you show that you belong by always being inclusive.   This attitude also has its unfortunate side.   It reveals that acceptance is rated as a higher virtue above truth. The desire to please others by accepting them lacks the backbone which will ask the hard questions.

REDUCTIONIST MYTHS

Having looked at questions of background and temperament and the way they influence attitude, we now turn to the way we use certain words and phrases. We have all heard people argue that 'the problem is nothing but . . . ' It is a useful device to simplify a complicated argument. However, usually there is a deliberate sleight of hand, since this is not just a simplification, but an over-simplification. When we say 'the problem is nothing but . . . ', we may well be deliberately dismissing other important facts. In fact, you can rarely *reduce* complicated issues to just one factor. There are shades of understanding that need to be revealed.

In the ecumenical debate there are at least three areas where we need to recognise that there is an inherent complexity.   Reductionism will not do!

1.   Levels of communication

If we are to avoid misunderstanding between the anti-ecumenical and pro-ecumenical mind, we need to rescue the words 'communication' and 'dialogue' from being 'nothing but' dirty words. Communication is almost always a good thing; it does not indicate 'agreement'. Similarly, 'dialogue' is not a dirty word: for example, Evangelism means dialogue! We are *all* engaged in communication and dialogue at *some* level - the words are neutral. This issue is simply *where* we put the balance in ecumenical debate.

2. Levels of administration

One of the most confusing aspects of the ecumenical debate is the way Christians can argue for and against an issue, not realising that they are confusing different levels of inter-church administration. What might be 'nothing but' a bad thing at a local level may nevertheless have something to commend it at a national level - or vice versa. To avoid misunderstanding we need to understand at which level/s of co-operation people are seeking to encourage ecumenical dialogue. For example, at a national level the media may ask for a response 'from the churches' on political, social and ethical issues. On some issues like homelessness, pornography and the arms trade, churches can speak with a common mind. Consultation and co-operation between denominations is clearly desirable. At the local level there may also be political and moral issues to deal with. There may also be opportunities of working together in worship and mission. It is the right-or wrongness of types of co-operation at specific levels that has to be debated, rather than adopting blanket positions, come what may. The point is this: different levels of church administration require different rationales. We should not reduce all dialogue and co-operation to 'nothing but' evil.

3. Levels of co-operation

Not only do we need to distinguish levels of administration but also the sorts of area of co-operation. The two issues are obviously very closely linked. Working together with other churches can be at all sorts of levels. There may be:

* *social co-operation*, e.g., working together to ban a local sex shop or to highlight the problem of homelessness;
* *worship co-operation*, e.g., an Easter march or Christmas united witness;
* *Evangelistic co-operation*, e.g., a town-wide mission.

Misunderstanding occurs when we have not distinguished the level of co-operation we are actually talking about. It is, therefore, unhelpful to say that all co-operation is 'nothing but' a hindrance to the Gospel. Everyone will sanction *some* level of co-operation.

4 Levels of truth

It is on issues of truth that the ecumenical debate becomes most serious. We may do things differently because of varied histories, but when a fundamental Christian truth in another group is at variance with the way we see things, then we cannot but take careful notice. We may feel very strongly about a question of revealed truth, but we must concede that there are levels of truth. Some principles we will want to defend passionately, without compromise, but there are other issues about which we are prepared to live with other people's differences. Issues of truth are discussed elsewhere in this symposium but these are some guidelines:

Primary truths would include:

> Christ: his divine person and atoning work.
> Salvation: by grace through faith.
> Authority: the inspiration and full authority of Scripture.
> Church: made up of believers who gather together.

Secondary Truths would include:

> Precise type of church government.
> Precise way of Christ's second coming.
> Baptism - where Evangelicals clearly disagree and yet co-operate.

When we meet with other church groups we need to be sure that the issues of truth we defend are worth defending. It is unfortunate and misleading when all questions of doctrine and practice are lumped together as 'nothing but' fundamental truth!

PROBLEMS OF PLURALISM AND GUILT BY ASSOCIATION

For the anti-ecumenical mind the problem of guilt by association is a key issue. It is argued that *any* involvement with a Christian body that has compromised the Gospel brings guilt. Moreover, it is argued that such co-operation is confusing to the outsider and to young Christians. They will ask 'if you think Gospel truths are worth fighting for, why do you have even a distant link with a body that isn't clear about the Gospel?' In an age where there is so much syncretism, pluralism and toleration, many Christians feel 'twitchy' about co-operation that seems to blur important distinctives.

Despite the high sounding goals of the above thesis, there are several problems. Firstly, where does the question of guilt by association stop? Is there to be separation on primary or secondary levels? For example, we can imagine church 'A' linked with church 'B' because they are totally united on truth; but if it is discovered that church 'B' has some loose links with church 'C' (which is a bit suspect about the Gospel) is it impossible for 'A' and 'B' to have fellowship together?

Secondly, if you are quite clear about where you stand with regard to truth, why is it that loose assocation with another makes you guilty? If it is publicly made clear that you do not approve of certain aspects, then surely you have no guilt! There is guilt only if you condone plurality yourself or condone plurality in others. To put it another way, if you make your position clear and (verbally) disassociate from those who are pluralists, then you have no guilt. 'We may be unpopular bedfellows but we are not guilty.' (Amess). Finally, it ought to be recognised that the Baptist view of the independence of the local church is also a reason why the charge of 'guilt by association' is invalid. No outside body (whether it is the Baptist Union or an ecumenical body) can dictate to a local Baptist in matters of faith and practice. This independence will mean that there is always the safeguard against compromise at local level.

PASSAGES OF SCRIPTURE WHICH SPEAK TO BOTH ECUMENICAL MINDS

So far we have not put our thinking under the rule of Scripture. In fact, Scripture speaks to both mind sets with the need to pursue unity in the framework of truth.

* John 17 reminds us of our Lord's great desire for unity among the disciples. He longed for a unity that reflected the very nature of the Godhead. However, it was to be a unity based on truth.

* 1 Cor 12: 12-13 reminds us that unity is not just a hope for the future but a present experience. In other words, we already have Christian unity

among true believers. Structural unity between churches is a different issue.

* The Apostle of Love reminds us in his letter (1 John) that there are only three grounds on which separation is valid. He therefore applies a moral test, a social (love) test and a doctrinal test. We should be careful that we do not separate on issues that Scripture does not countenance. In closing. we should all note that the New Testament has as much to say about the sin of schism as it does about the error of compromise (Phil 2, Titus 3:9-11, Rom 16:17).

ANDREW RIGDEN-GREEN